About the Author

Christina Rose is exceptionally boring. She has just been flung into fairly exceptional circumstances. As an artist, she feels moved to tell her story of overcoming mental illness. She will always live with bipolar disorder, as much as this book will always live with her. If it even helps one person, she would be delighted. In many ways, it is written to her younger self. Be good.

A Long Way from Home

Christina Rose

A Long Way from Home

Olympia Publishers
London

www.olympiapublishers.com
OLYMPIA PAPERBACK EDITION

A CIP catalogue record for this title is
available from the British Library.

ISBN: 978-1-80439-780-0

This book is memoir. It reflects the author's present recollections of
experiences over time. Some names and characteristics have been
changed, some events have been compressed, and some dialogue
has been recreated.

First Published in 2024

Olympia Publishers
Tallis House
2 Tallis Street
London
EC4Y 0AB

Printed in Great Britain

Dedication

I dedicate this book to my friends and family. In particular, my mum.

PREFACE

Where to begin? From which point to depart in a long line of misadventures, near scrapes, and fairly kaleidoscopic visual contortions of stays in various psychiatric units? The only way back is to follow the breadcrumbs, in my very own version of a Brothers Grimm fairy tale, right back to the start. The moment I received the label that, all at once, made sense of a nonsensical life, and at the same time shook the foundations of who I was, like a gust of cold wind blasting through the scaffolding of a person made up of what was then seemingly nothing more than just a projection.

So we will begin with a jolt right back at that instant when my world was ripped apart, and so attempt to resurrect the person from before, or as we find her, perhaps bid her a fond farewell over our shoulders as she becomes just another ghost in the rear view mirror…

CHAPTER 1
Please Don't Ruin My Life

I often trip over words or fail to keep pace with what I am thinking, my mind works at a quickstep tempo and my fingers and lack of dexterity (unpractised since I gave up my piano lessons as a teenager) tend to fall short of catching up in time. I often end up metaphorically wheezing out sentences as I write when the words and ideas form in my mind at a pace which is sometimes hard to keep up with or narrow down. I must also give a heads up, that I tend to meander. For me, writing is about going on a journey through various different thoughts and visual landscapes which I see and pass by, perusing like a tourist events from the past, and I see my experiences as little vignettes, a pastiche of various different visual scenarios as if painted on a canvas. I am often transported in my mind's eye, back in time, whether I want to visit it or not, and these little visitations will pop up, spring up on me from behind like a leering stranger, and tap me on the shoulder. All of a sudden, I am back to where it all began. I am back amongst it all, in the thick of it as it were, even if in a diluted version of events.

The way that I write is in many ways a disorganised map of memories as they present themselves to me. Therefore, I should forewarn you, the reader, to abandon any expectation of a narrow chronological order. I understand that to be a successful writer, one must present ideas in a linear series. Things just make sense in that way. But not much of my life, or my experience of it, does in fact make a lot of sense. So in true form, I am going to just ad lib the majority of my recounting, and extend apologies in advance. How I see my past is in fact much like flipping through an old family album, familiar faces here and there, times spent wrapped in love and glorified in nostalgia, as well as time slowed down to a minimal pace, where the slow ticking of the minute hand on the clock of my life felt achingly slow. I have been there, trapped in the purgatory of life, where everything shuts down and you are left alone with nothing but yourself, your thoughts and your nightmares. Which is where I think I will choose to begin. You know how fun a game it is to spin a globe and put a pin on a country when it stops circling in a dizzying motion on its stand? That is much the approach with which I will attempt to write my existence into your experience. In doing so, going along this journey hand in hand, like ramblers on an isolated mountain path, maybe I too, will find who I am, and this is certainly one of the reasons for writing this book.

I think I shall start at the point from which I remember disintegrating. Of course, not everybody ends up waking up in a psychiatric unit, and the phenomenon of being there is not really an open subject. I think it would be appropriate to set the scene, in order that you, dear reader, are able to form an image in your mind. I do not wish for the image you conjure up from me recounting to stay with you in the same vivid manner that it does with me. I experience memories in flashes, a series of images that almost flicker in front of me, obscuring my real time vision, swooping me back to the past from which I am always trying to run. One particularly strong image that I try to strictly avert my mind from, is the one I refer to as 'the one with the scratch-marks on the wall.' As with most things in life, efficiency is a wonderful thing and I would say that this memory is named as such because it describes exactly what it refers to. It does what it says on the tin, if you will. But seeing scratch marks on a wall is much like seeing hieroglyphics carved into the tombs of pharaohs - it is the story and narrative behind the marks that should be paid attention to.

I first saw scratch marks on the wall when I woke up from a heavy and drug-glazed sleep on my second admission to a psychiatric unit. I was lying on a blue plastic mattress, a few inches deep, with an NHS issued blanket wrapped around my body. Those scratch marks were inscribed right next to where my head laid on the pillow, so it was all I could do to turn over and not face the wall. What those marks represented, was a visual representation of someone from before, and I knew that they did not bode well for me, marooned here in this little room, slowly widening my eyes to the confines of my surroundings.

So, visually, the alphabet of fear and mental illness was written down, as if a billboard advertisement for someone warning me, a realisation of some kind of mental apparition, instructing me that I was not in a good place. I was not safe, this was not going to be an easy ride and I was going to have to get used to these scratch marks, made as if initials of someone in extreme distress. These lines dragged down the cream-coloured wall were an alphabet of a universal language. Much like the Cyrillic alphabet, which I find beautiful to look at, we cannot decipher it if we come from an English language background. It is foreign to us. However, scratches on a wall transcend normal methods of communication, you understand what they mean, you feel the energy that is left over in the creases of the marks, of a person in sheer and utter anguish.

So, I knew from these scratch marks on the wall that I was in a place of suffering. As my eyes adjusted to my surroundings, detaching from those indelible marks dragged down by somebody from before, I registered the sparse contents of my room. A table, a chair, a cupboard, a window. This is where I was to be for an unknown amount of time. This was to be my home from home, this was to be my cell. Years later in therapy, I got a stern telling off by a particular therapist who tutted at my propensity to refer to it as such. She had a tendency to shake her head and mutter at me that I was not, in fact, in a jail. I was not, in fact, in a dungeon. I was in fact, holed up in a safe unit of a psychiatric ward and I should be grateful for even having been allocated a bed on such a ward given the prevalence of mental illness at that time. But for me, I still feel it preferable to refer to it as a cell. We were, to all intents and purposes, locked in at all times, free to roam the quarters of our barracks during the day. Well, more or less, and to a certain extent. Much to my inconvenience, permission had to be obtained from a member of staff to be allowed outside for a cigarette. To get a whiff of fresh air one needed to have express consent and then be watched at all times, whilst puffing down and swallowing that smoke, that blessed nicotine that seemed the only recourse to unwinding, for a brief and fleeting moment. Now, I don't know if you have ever had a cigarette whilst being keenly observed, but it is all rather self-conscious and makes the whole process a whole lot more faff and palaver than it is worth. I would race the glowing amber of the cigarette from its tip to its base, trying to get the whole mechanical process over with as quickly as possible, as I felt so uncomfortable.

I digress, where was I? So I shall rewind back to the picture you might have by now formed in your mind, of my visual surroundings. As far as a blueprint for what my bedroom looked like at least. But as we know, our phenomenological experience of life is not only what we see but what we hear. What we listen to, or choose not to listen to or what we feel in vibrations. And so, an adequate description of where we are in this stage of the introduction, must therefore include the sounds. The 3-D effect of being on a unit, for in my experience, what we hear is far more difficult to block out than what we see. Anybody can close their eyes, can squint them shut, can turn away from a bloody scene if squeamish, can block out that which we choose not to witness.

With sounds, they penetrate through airwaves in such a motion that even sticking our fingers into our ears and screwing up our faces, willing away the noises, they kind of still permeate. It only makes you feel as if you are underwater, obscuring the sounds which alarm you, and the sounds, the rhythm of those airwaves, the garbled truths of the people around me in that unit, are what stay with me more than the visual imprint.

It would start at night, when the lights went out. Just at the moment when the script of evening medication was about to kick in and lay you into a pseudo coma, then it would start. A wail, more than that, a deep and guttural moan. High-pitched, gurgling out words and sexually explicit vocabulary. Like a siren on the rocks, or someone blowing a distress whistle lost out at sea, her cries would begin and not cease for hours. It became routine. During the day, this girl, heart-crushingly beautiful and young, would appear even 'normal', perhaps reticent, but not recognisable or comparable to the screaming chorus that would begin as night encroached.

I don't know what became of her. I often think of her. I hope she has found some resolution or something approaching a sense of peace. But she is only one of many ghosts which I remember from my time spent, where we all had to divulge our blood and guts to a doctor once a week. Where we all tried to evade the system, to formulate plots in order to crack our way out of the psych ward, much as if we were on a game show like the Crystal Maze. We all had that in common: none of us wanted to be there but we were all heaped amongst each other, strangers, and yet not unfamiliar with the one thing we all knew, the unifying yet unedifying spectre of Suffering.

I would like to digress, if I might, into including in this chapter some of the other characters that I came across who have left an impact on me, whom I remember still now, nearly a decade on. I do not remember names, which is quite alright in this case, as for the purposes of anonymity and personal data protection it is only appropriate. I do however, have a knack for faces, and episodes in the timeline of my visual memory play out in front of me as if I am watching a TV programme. What I find incorrect and rather intolerable about the perception of mental illness in society, is the notion that mentally ill people are in fact mentally decrepit. A busted flush. Mentally handicapped, incapable, and without recourse to intelligence. This, I know from experience, could not be further from the truth and reality.

For instance, I will bring up a lady from my last stay in a psychiatric ward, after an ill thought out, embarrassingly planned and mistaken suicide attempt. I had spilt a load of paracetamol out onto my bed, and swallowed them one by one like jelly tots, counting until I got to the tally of sixteen, at which point I reached for my mobile phone and swung a call to a trusted friend, expressing what I had just done, much to my shame at the melodrama of the whole situation.

She promptly advised that I get to hospital, and as I lived within walking distance, I agreed and shuffled each mortified step down to A&E, where I met her straight from her work, and was seen by the psychiatric consultant. Being so highly

15

embarrassed by my actions, I tried to talk my way out of being admitted. I reeled out all the likely excuses, regurgitating what I am sure everybody who attempts to escape, even temporarily, the haze of their emotional distress, must say. Possibly even verbatim. The doctor was having none of it, and after staying for an assessment, where for a split second I wondered if I had jeopardised my kidneys or some other major internal organ, I was given the all clear, except for the fact that I would have to stay in the psychiatric unit whilst the rest of my mental health was inspected, observed and so on.

And so, it happened that I landed up on the ward where I met the lady I am about to bring into this story. I actually saw her many years later, out in the community at the same mental health clinic where I was an outpatient. She looked much better, very much like she had in the ward but reassuringly calmer. Seeing her jogged my memory and I gave her an knowing look from across the room as I left my appointment. Not a smile as such, not even much but a passing acknowledgement, a certain expression of, 'I remember you, and I remember what we have both been through.' It gave me a sense of coming full circle, and led me to experience a feeling of hope, that not all who struggle are lost for good.

So, to return to the earlier point from which I departed on a wander to the more recent past, delving back into my time spent on this particular ward, I will describe this lady as I found her at that time. Being on a ward, you quickly adjust, because you have to, you must, in order to be able to survive the pressure and be on your toes, keeping your wits about you, as for certain you never know the background of the other patients. It is all very confidential and you have to trust your gut instinct and be aware of a microscopic level of detail at all times. This sounds a lot like paranoia, especially as people living through the most difficult time of their lives, and people suffering with mental illness in general, are not likely to be dangerous. That is a terrible myth perpetuated by strands of the media and society, and one which I will attempt to dispel and hope to dismantle over the course of this book. However, the ward was a mixed ward, with strictly separate male and female sleeping quarters of course. We had shared shower facilities, and the main door at the end of the corridor was locked at night, we were effectively bolted in.

But during the day, we all would mingle together, masquerading at a normal life with scheduled activities, be they art therapy, music, film nights, all broken up by the routine of receiving medication three times a day, after meal times. Meal times are an interesting topic that I will return to later, but I want to focus on this lady, who I shall call Diana.

Diana had a vast and almost encyclopaedic knowledge of politics. She was like a walking, talking Daily Telegraph. She would have expressly lucid moments, where she would rail against the injustices and pick apart the political landscape with adept authority. She would leave me agog at the reach of her information recall, given that we had limited access to the world outside the ward, except for the use of our mobile phones or laptops when it was allowed during the day. Which is another thing in fact: much to my annoyance, because of the circumstances surrounding my admission into the ward, and given my history of two previous stays in a psychiatric unit, I was not permitted to have my laptop charging cable in my room overnight. It was part of protocol, as obviously the grim reality was that the cord could be used as a makeshift ligature, which was assessed as unsafe for me given the circumstances of my admission.

Listening to Diana, therefore, was much like listening to a babbling radio in the background, reciting clearly thought out, logical, and impressively developed monologues on what she imagined we do about the state of the country. When she was lucid, one would assume she were a high-level civil servant or some other professional. The cruelty dealt to her was her fixation and belief that she was in immediate mortal danger as a result of damage to her kidneys. Much of the day would involve Diana swooping along the corridor, pacing about the main lounge, crying out desperately that she was going to die. Repetition along that theme was reality, this was her reality, and we all experienced it on a daily basis.

There is another character I wish to venerate within these pages and my tale of life on the psych ward, someone who made an impression on me that I will never forget. The meal times I referred to earlier, to describe them as they were, were the worst times of the day. A ceremonial affair of dreary food, aimless queuing and then silent chewing, all of us not quite sure what to say to the person sat opposite, as each wipe clean table was spaced out so as to accommodate two people. I mostly didn't want to make friends. I didn't delve into much conversation during these rather excruciating times, gulping down whatever lay in front of me, watched all the time to make sure I was eating, as another problem at the time was the weight I had lost from not eating. The first thing to go when you have depression is your appetite. In all honesty, since those days I have never really fully recovered my appetite. I rarely finish a meal, much to my embarrassment, and playing roulette with my eating has detrimentally affected my metabolism.

To bring in this next card of the pack, who we shall call John, I should probably initiate the reader into his condition. Now, as you will discover over the course of the next chapters, I have a diagnosis of bipolar disorder, considered a 'trendy' mental illness, on account of so many well-known celebrities having received the same diagnosis. I will dedicate a chapter to my interpretation of the rather confounding and silly 'one size fits all' approach to living with this debilitating condition, but for now let us keep aim on John.

I was instantly smitten with John, a man I would gauge was somewhere between his fifties and sixties, grey hair, dishevelled outfit, glint in his eye and an easy smile. One day, he came over to my table, where he would have found me staring nonchalantly down into the plastic plate, divided into sections for hot meal, drink, fruit, etc. I was probably aimlessly trying to quieten the reality of where I was and what I could feel I was losing, which was a grip on my reality and past. It is extremely difficult to eat with an aching sense of depression. It is one of the most laborious of chores to nourish what you do not value. When you do not feel particularly like pursuing life or goals or anything in particular, eating is an act of extreme punishment. Yet we must eat. We must eat in order for the meds we are served as dessert to be able to action their release, so that at least at the end of the day, we will be able to drop off to sleep.

And so, John found me one day. He bounced and nearly crash landed onto the seat opposite me, and instantly struck up a conversation. I say conversation, but you must understand that I was practically mute at the time, not willing to exert myself over anything else but getting the meal over with so that I could retreat into my little room, with the scratch marks on the wall. John, as I must have mentioned earlier, had a diagnosis of bipolar disorder, and boy, did he have a textbook case of it! I believe that he was in a state of mania when he introduced himself to me that time. Having been manic myself, years earlier, so much so that I actually lost all touch with reality and ended up in a whirlwind of a psychotic episode which concluded in me believing that I was in fact God, I could detect the signs I knew so well in myself. Gibberish. They call it 'flight of ideas', the professionals. The momentum with which John talked, as if extinguishing an inner sense of turmoil, with words tumbling out of his mouth, pouring out onto the plastic plate of food beneath him.

'You don't say very much do you?' he mentioned, acknowledging my presence that I was trying to maintain as invisible, as if he was trying to coax me out of the sluggish sense of doom which I felt as a heavy presence. He began explaining how he was a poet, joy and rhymes mixed up in his sentences as he talked to me. I didn't say very much at that time. That much was true. It was a very physical feeling of numbness, or blankness, or just a great emptiness which I can only describe as a feeling of feeling so bereft and so exhausted and so overwhelmingly disappointed, that I just did not have the energy to commit to engaging with anything or anyone in the world I found myself. John was the first person to attempt to engage me since I had been there. He effectively broke into my personal space and made himself appear, made himself known, and made me feel a sense of connection.

Of all the above surveyed, I have given a glimpse of an overview, firstly starting with the shiniest memories I hold, that flit across my windscreen every so often, and there are many more to come. Of course, my own personal story is one we will delve into in due course. I can reassure the reader that I was not desolately alone throughout my various internments at hospital. I actually had a boyfriend during those most turbulent years, who I shall introduce as we Segway our route, zigzagging hither and thither. But I like to handle memories as they fall off of the tip of my tongue. Writing them out before they disappear and vanish, escaping into the past from which they came, from which I have spent years hiding from.

As an artist, I am a visual thinker. It is not a choice, it is not a handicap, it is just the way my brain is wired. As far as logical thinking, that is completely out of the window, I just am left to overcompensate by strenuously dallying around with pictures in my head. This method of thinking, how I am wired upstairs, is the reason I am an artist, and it is no coincidence that I picked up a degree in art history before going on to pursue fine art at art school, before entering into the world of fashion as a dogsbody-cum-stylist assistant.

A symptom or side effect of thinking visually is that I sustain imagery for years in some kind of repository in my brain. I also struggle with extremely vivid dreams. Or, more aptly put, nightmares. The extraordinary element of finding yourself confined in a unit for mentally ill folk, is how perplexing it is to be confronted by visions of a real nightmare scape, and how essentially normal and mundane they appear. How you do not tend to even react to images that would wake you up from your bad dream in a state of shock. The unfolding of a living nightmare is how some people describe traumatic events, and I would also, as I find that an appropriate description. Suddenly, your existence is in a phantasmagorical world, shrunken into a locked space inhabited by people you know nothing about, and monitored constantly by the unflinching gaze of the staff on site.

If you would allow me, and humour the way I catapult from recent to older experiences, I suppose I do so as a means to express just how jumbled up my own internal mindscape appears to me. There are lurid images that stand out to me, and bring

21

themselves to the forefront of my memory as I sift through the bank of them. And there is one, if you do not mind and allow me to indulge myself, in order to excoriate myself from the trauma, that I would like to explain to you, reader.

It was during what I would describe as my first 'stay' in a psych unit, as I never really count the first time, when I had a nervous breakdown and spent the night in hospital before being discharged, which was rather a regrettable mistake. I was extremely unwell, having had a housemate call me an ambulance as I was found wandering aimlessly about the local park, setting forth a rather wild goose chase for my whereabouts, as I had last been spotted by a concerned member of the public, singing and spitting out unintelligible poetry.

I was convinced I was the female reincarnation of Jesus and that I was communing with God directly as his conduit on Earth. I was in the throes of a massive psychotic episode and experiencing the unsettling symptom of auditory hallucinations. I digress, and I assure you that I will go into the details of the onset of my breakdowns and everything in between in due course, but in this opening chapter, I aim to signal to my strongest and heaviest memories first, in order to get them out of the way. So, given the fact that I think visually, and my memory is made up of a series of three dimensional diagrams, an image I would like to get off my chest is probably the most disturbing one I wish I could unsee.

It is an image of a deep, angry, red line. Red is a difficult colour for me. It is very symbolic of blood, it is of course used by teachers to mark the mistakes in school childrens' work, it is the colour of piping hot flames, it is the colour people use to describe when they fly into a rage. "I saw red, Guv." A final character for this chapter, before I move on to fill out the gaps I have left so far with metaphorical polyfiller, is one I shall refer to as Stacey.

It was near the end of my stay on the ward, where I had been for a few days, as I was assessed and diagnosed with bipolar disorder, and as my episode of mania gradually wore off and I levelled out to the next horrifying segment of the illness: the crashing reality of depression and horror and feeling mortified as you begin to come to terms with the reality that you have just lost your mind, and all that entails, and now you have to explain away the crippling humiliation of not actually being the reincarnation of Jesus on Earth, and instead just a very ill young lady.

I felt okay, given the circumstances, as I was being discharged. Discharged to then become an outpatient of the local mental health in the community team, under whose care I would remain for quite a few years to come. But the important thing to me at that time was that to some extent, I was being awarded my freedom. I was free to go; go where and where onto next was quite another thing to organise or even contemplate, but I was not going to boxed off to another ward on the hospital grounds, from which I imagined escape would be near impossible. I wondered if the screaming girl next to me in the sleeping quarters was to be admitted to one of the more permanent wards. I think I remember enquiring and being informed that yes, indeed, she was going to be staying longer term. Anyway, any sense of comradeship I had fostered with the other patients was waning, and in a relatively upbeat mood, all things considered, I looked about me for somewhere to count down the hours until I was allowed to exit officially. As a matter of fact, this took much prodding, and I would ask every hour or so for an indication of when I was allowed to leave, my few belongings all packed up, a sense of uncertainty that I would actually be allowed out, and a matching

23

sense of dread in the pit of my stomach that it might all be a dreadful mistake and I may have to endure another night in the unit.

Anyway, happily, in the end I was indeed allowed to walk out and catch a bus home to my quiet house share in Wood Green, North London. Riding the bus looking, I'm sure, much like an escaped convict, it was a pretty memorable journey... with which I can come to explain my aversion to the colour red. It was during that waiting time, rather like purgatory, or the waiting room Dr Seuss writes about in my favourite of his childhood classics, 'Oh, the places you'll go', I came across Stacey. Much like with John, I was in a state of semi-mania, not quite revved enough to remain committed or sectioned, yet still oscillating at a buzzing frequency, rather energised by the chemical cocktail that had ravaged my brain some days previously. I saw Stacey sat down; she too was waiting. I seem to remember that, as the unit I was on was a short-stay unit, it was routine to have people moved on or out at the end of the week. And it must have been the end of the week that we found ourselves sitting opposite each other, each privately facing an unknowable future. I began talking. I opened my mouth and I introduced myself. Mania does funny things to your sense of inhibitions, as they otherwise evaporate, and this is the manner in which I found myself trying to make small talk with Stacey.

Stacey looked sad. Not just sad but devastated sad. Weary, tired, eyes devoid of any glimmer. This was not from the expression on her face, which was pretty blank as far as I remember, but the expression of her eyes. It was on those sad circles that I focused, round and unblinking, looking through me as I rattled off whichever inane nonsense came to mind. I had been looking into that gaze intently, so much so that it took me a

24

little while to cast my eyes elsewhere, upon what was a round but pretty, and desperately young, face. At what I saw next, I sort of jolted, sat up straight in my chair, alarmed and shocked, and all at once, I felt like crying. What I saw, as my own eyes cast around, was Stacey's neck. And suddenly it all made sense. I mean, that turn of phrase is a careless one, a loose train of thought, as of course none of it made any sense at all. If anything, it made sense seem impossible. How I had missed it, I kicked myself, a deep red, angry straight line cut across her pale neck, standing out as if to scream at me, 'How could you not see how much I hurt?'

Once I had noticed the ligature mark, I made a feeble attempt to carry on the momentum of the conversation I had initiated. I tried to stop staring at the gash, or thinking of what can only be explained as a very recent suicide attempt. Raw pain. I was sat opposite a sign and symbol of real human pain and suffering, and Stacey needn't have said anything at all, as the gash across her throat said everything she needed to. It is one of the saddest moments of my life involving another person. Frightening, and deeply violent, but an image that I cannot shake from my memories. And it unfolded in real time, over nearly ten years ago, and yet as vividly as anything, that saturated red line marks a line between my past life up until that point, and the life I was about to commence, navigating my future while negotiating my diagnosis of bipolar disorder.

CHAPTER 2
An Unfortunate Set of Circumstances

And so, dear reader, as I have flourished my fancy at a variety of memories to set the scene, in order to prepare you for the journey we will both be making, a backdrop, a bit of set design if you will, which we can use as a reference point, all of the happenings that I have so far covered, are occurrences that came to be as a result of something else.

This chapter promises to be a gut-wrenching one for me, and my stamina to process what I shield myself from with the myriad substances available, which people have used over time to quash and numb the salient feelings and conflicted emotions which sometimes take us off-kilter. There is always an explanation for somebody to be found in the circumstances of abusing whichever variety of intoxicant they can lay their hands on. Each person, or addict as we call them, as we shortcut any kind of personalisation and construct these damaged humans into a depersonified, remote object. People are easier to reflect back what we are afraid of within ourselves when we are able to reduce them to being robotic. When we blame them and cajole them, when we denigrate them as somewhat less than us, somewhat unholy, somewhat part of an unknowable mass of the unwashed. As soon as you label a person as an addict, you negate any responsibility to have a sense of empathy or compassion with said person. Because it's frightening, right? Me, I am frightened by the nihilistic ways how people afflicted with addiction operate. A sense of recklessness in not wanting to pursue a responsible life, a sense of chaos, and a sense of alarm that I myself might be pulled down into such a path, such a dangerous spiral from which I may never resurface.

Perhaps addiction, and my own struggles with alcohol, will be something I go further into detail about later on in this book. But as with much of the time, it is in fact only a red herring, and a decoy used to deflect from the actual illness I carry. From the actual condition I endure on a daily basis. It is not alcoholism that I struggle with, rather it is the far weightier burden of manic depression, and everything tied up in that.

As with everything, there is a beginning. With the onset of bipolar disorder, there is usually a traumatic event or series of traumatic events that lead up to the unfavourable circumstances of a toxic internal storm. There are agents in what leads that house of cards to fall, an event or a person who topples that first domino. This is the chapter in which I will lay out my reasoning of the why, the who and the how. I suspect that it will be the most difficult chapter for me to construct, and certainly not easy to read or digest. I will try my hardest not to skirt away from that which still scares me to this day. It is very scary as a prospect, to write what in some cases could have been written out in a suicide note. So, I herein insert a trigger warning for those of a sensitive predisposition, and feel free to skip this chapter, as it already feels suffocating for me, the writer, and I haven't even begun it yet.

It was a rape. Rape. Sexual assault. Call it what you will. Rape is such an ugly word. No more applicable word could be used to term such an horrific thing. In my life story, it wasn't the first time that it had happened to me. The first time was at a party, an old school friend's 21st birthday, to which I had tried to avoid going, yet at which he very much assured me that I was on the top table, and I had to be there. That time wasn't so bad. It was, it was awful in actual fact, gynaecological almost. It happened in the back of a car in a field. I had said no; even whilst it was happening I was repeating, no. Words don't really carry much significance in the face of an assault by somebody with a sense of conviction and lack of remorse. I do remember saying no. I remember the deadly silence in the car journey back up to university the next day, whilst I was in shock, my inner monologue absolute hysterical, processing what had occurred the previous night.

I say that it was not THIS rape, in particular, that was devastating. I shelved it. I resumed life as normal and never told anybody. Except for my boyfriend at that time, to whom I had to explain what had happened. Anyway, much of a muchness, time passed and it lessened and I was able to finish my studies at university without it having too large of a detrimental effect. I just made the conscious decision to park it, to never revisit it and to write it off as a bad experience.

Already, I was laying down the path of minimising fairly cataclysmic life events, and this would indeed come back to haunt me in a rather big way, as we shall see.

The thing wot did me in, as they say, is the second time it happened. This time, later on in life, it was far more difficult to swallow down and move on from. And goes some way to explaining what precipitated my fall down the rabbit hole into mental illness.

The difficult thing about rape, and being a rape victim or rape survivor, according to which lexicon you feel more comfortable with to frame the exact same thing, is its knock-on effects. It is not so much the physical act, which is obviously frightening and painful and paralysing, but the mental act of deviance and betrayal that scars your ability to trust in people. For me personally, the actual act did not take very long at all, yet the effects lasted for over a decade and surely still resonate with me today. Most likely, the sad truth is that they will reverberate with me for the rest of my life. It is in the taking of something that is unquantifiable and intangible and utterly irreplaceable. Another person took something from me that I will never be able to get back, some unreachable sense of self, my potential, my dreams and my concept of what the world is. I by no means believed that I was living in Disneyland, and was well aware of the cruel reality of life in many respects, but rape is an act of burglary. There is no getaway driver, there is no way to claim compensation, and there is no insurance company that you can contact to cover the costs.

So, there in my own story, and how I came to find myself in a psychiatric unit, with this new-fangled term 'bipolar disorder', something which I had never really heard of in my preceding twenty-five years, is a rape. And with a deep breath, we must rid ourselves of feeling self-conscious or ashamed or embarrassed as I so very often do, and venture into the realities of that, not expecting to feel any sense of relief, as I have tried to attain that with much therapy and find it impossible. You cannot relive the past and you cannot undo what is done to you. You can only testify to it as your truth, and hope that it might help as a form of catharsis to document, or even alleviate the fear for somebody else to whom it happened, who is still afraid. And, trust me, I am still afraid.

I was staying with a friend from university. I say friend, but he was always a bit of an oddball. I never particularly gravitated towards him and our social circles were radically different. I was orbiting around a crowd of public boarding school kids, who put on raves in their spare time. These raves were unimaginatively called Cave Raves, Craves, as they took place in the caves on the university campus. They happened every once in a while, with an abundance of joy, and glitter, and pixies made out of papier mache. I was in love for the first time in my life with one of the founders. That was my crowd and they were my people. Perhaps later on, I can take the liberty of digressing into that period of joy and liberation, but for now it is probably best to stay on topic.

So, I was staying with a friend from university in London, finding my lacklustre post-uni life down in Dorset with my mother, in the remote middle of the countryside, stifling. I would later be kicked out by my mother, which is of course something else to approach somewhere along the line. I had previously sold a painting to this man, whom I referred to as a friend, and had in my mind that he was trustworthy. So much so, that I had consensual sex with him. More out of pity than anything else, as the attraction on my side was simply not there. He had a strange thing about him that I perceived even then. So I was, in many ways, remiss to have a pity shag with him. However, I did. On one occasion prior, he had invited me to a private viewing at the Tate Britain, which I accompanied him to, and I took time out to show and explain to him the semiotics of my favourite painting at the time, *The Great Day Of His Wrath*, by John Martin. It is not for nothing that I had spent three years training in art history, and I am able to wax lyrical when art and imagery is the subject matter and open to interpretation.

A rather painful consequence of what would eventually transpire, is that I cannot bear to even look at this painting any more. He also took that away from me, my favourite painting. Now when I look at it, I instantly jolt, even if it pops up on a

Facebook newsfeed or in an article, as it so often does, particularly a few years ago when there was a massive retrospective of the body of work of John Martin. It is a reminder of him, him and his hold and purveyance of power and domination over me, and that evening that I explained my thoughts on my favourite work of art. Now when I see it, briefly, at a glance, all I see is this man's face and remember that night and all that happened after that unfortunate series of events.

How my rape transpired, in its gory lack of violence, was during my sleep. I woke up in the middle of it. Having gone to bed fully clothed, and passed out, I woke up in the middle of being assaulted in the darkness. That evening, this man had been out at a work event, and prior to him leaving me in peace for that evening, he had told me a bit of an autobiographical spiel about how his mother had left, she had either left or she had committed suicide, I don't remember which it was. It was all rather sad and tragic.

When he left, I decided to have a drink or three, before plummeting into bed and giving up the ghost. Anyway, this is a very difficult chapter to write and I don't see what purpose it serves particularly. I don't feel a sense of peace but rather I feel as if I am back there, in that room, the weight of another body on top of me in the darkness.

I do not wish to go into further details, as it is overall an unpleasant memory to situate myself in, but it would explain what happened next over the next six months of my life.

'Please don't ruin my life!' he screamed out as I winced, running out of his flat. I hurtled into a taxi ordered for me by a friend I had rung, who directed me to jump in and head straight over to his house. Those eerie words still resonate with me today. I can hear the pitch, I can feel the fear.

Of course, an unpleasant aspect of the whole thing was the cliched element that he was a rich and politically connected man. He was involved with the Conservative Party, and I had on one occasion accompanied him to his gentlemen-only private members club in the heart of Mayfair for some godawful function. Heaven knows why I agreed to do that, but there we have it. This fits into my story of what happened next. Obviously, reader, I had run away in the middle of the night from this scene and what had just happened. I had left all of my belongings at his. Things as mundane but necessary as a bag of clothes and my hair straighteners. To get them back was essential. I consulted my friend who had rescued me that night, who eventually went on to become my boyfriend, and he said that he would act as a mediator. He was furious with this man, and insisted that he send over my remaining belongings to his house, where I was now staying, by courier or taxi.

Deviance is something unintelligible to those who are not that way inclined. But the malevolence with which this rapist acted next, blew my tiny little mind further. I was instructed to collect my belongings from the very same, hoity toity gentlemen-only members club in the heart of Mayfair, just around the corner from the Ritz. That this was an act of intimidation is so clear to me now, and perhaps was even then. I went along with the instructions. I took myself to Green Park and found the address, then asked the glamorous lady on reception for whichever locker number he had supplied, and took receipt of my bag, straighteners included.

With a sense of shock, I saw an envelope addressed to me. I opened it up. It was a Christmas card, from the man who had raped me days prior. For, of course, this was in the run up to Christmas. I instantly ripped up the card and threw it into a bin on the street. Feeling a sense of disgust, the likes of which I had

32

never experienced. And suddenly, given that I sometimes believe in serendipity, who do I bump into walking down this busy London street, but an old friend from the Crave crew, happily bouncing down the street carrying a leek under his arm. It was a complete joy to see his friendly face at that moment, bounding up to me as I was feeling kind of desolate.

All of this had an effect, in that I swore my friend to secrecy, never to tell anybody about what had taken place. I was terrified. Too scared to even go with the police to give a statement. I didn't really have the time to be a rape victim. I imagined that if I just shoved it all down, to an archaeological level, deep down, and never thought about it or remembered that it had happened, then I could wish it away and carry on with life as usual.

Which I did. Or, at least, I did for around six months, before one day at work, in my new job as a receptionist at the Virgin Media headquarters, flicking nonchalantly through Facebook, I came across as image of this man's face. It sent me into instantaneous free-fall. It precipitated what would become my enduring illness of bipolar disorder, and brought about the resurgence of my blocked memory, catalysing a violent bout of mania, which concluded in my total loss of touch with reality, and a psychotic episode.

So, when we look for a cause and effect, although there were many others, this is the cause that would end up in, rather than me ruining his life, as he begged me not to, in him ruining my life instead. Something which I find very difficult to come to terms with even to this day.

Thank you for bearing with me during this chapter, as that was really tough for me. And I hope that the remaining chapters will be much more conducive to reading. Some things, however, are not palatable, and that's just the way it is.

CHAPTER 3
Manic Depression

There is a reason why I prefer to use the term manic depression, in spite of it being discontinued today. It explains the reality of what my condition actually entails, and is much more descriptive than the commonly-used label of bipolar disorder.

My mental illness means that I suffer predominantly from a type of depression that is outside the range of normal experience, as perceived on a clinical level. Everybody feels depressed at some stage of their lives. Sad about the loss of a loved one, about physical health, about a dream or an ambition or any other life event which impacts on our mental health. We should all be very much aware of the spike in mental health referrals in recent years, as our whole nation collectively reels from over twelve years of austerity cuts, and world events outside of our control and far outside of our preferences unfold at a pace with which it is difficult to keep up. I am not alone in my illness by any means. But the dastardly thing about manic depression, in my personal experience, is the acuteness with which I feel it. A tugging sense of sadness and, to put it mildly, a pretty resolute sense of loss that permeates through every single moment of every single day.

For this reason, to alleviate the sensation of being about to drown psychologically, I tend to fall back on the coping mechanisms I have developed to cushion, or at least distract, from feeling that overwhelming sense of dread, fear and tiredness at life. As the last fifteen years of my life, the majority of my adult experience, have been very much based around trauma, I have had to find various escape routes so I am not left in that highly uncomfortable sense of flux. It is a physical sensation, the brand of sadness that I experience. I feel it as if it is a weighty cricket ball in the pit of my stomach, and all I can do to dispel the anxiety and sense of dread is to pick up a pencil and draw something. When I am drawing I do not think at all, but simply measure out shapes and tones and dimensions. It is an easy dance with a leaded pencil, across a page, translating in my visual handwriting an image as best I can.

It is a sense of compulsion therefore, to create art, and explains why I am so prolific in the amount I produce. It is an occasion for me to have a blank mind again, to thoroughly empty the horrible emotions which otherwise consume me in my solitude, and the end product also helps me to communicate with other people, from whom I otherwise feel very remote at times. It is a yearning to be understood by others, a feeling that I cannot explain how I feel emotionally, or the depths of despair I have lived through in my life, which make me feel marked out as somewhat different, unlovable, and essentially destined to be alone for the remainder of my life.

The sense that it is somehow impossible to translate how desolate I have felt and the sheer vastness of trauma I have experienced, compounds how distinct from other people I feel on a daily basis. I very much wish I was an uncomplicated version of a human being. I very much wish I had a simplistic outlook on life and did not have knowledge of what I have lived through. However this is not how things are, I am as much a product of my experiences as anybody, and that cannot be changed. Having said all of the above, and even with the excruciating pain and isolation I am familiar with, I would not choose to change the reality I inhabit, and the perception it has allowed me to gain as a result.

As a result of this outlook on life and the fierce consequences of living with this manic depression, I feel a real and earnest need to seek out beauty and beautiful things. Beautiful music, beautiful clothes, beautiful people, beautiful drawings. Anything to rub as a tonic on the wounds I otherwise feel stinging and throbbing inside of me. It is a terrible burden to endure the feeling of inner conflict and live with the reality of what has happened in my past. However on the flip side of that, wherein the bipolar label becomes relevant, I find it absolutely necessary to look at images and chase anything that takes me outside of myself and far away, into not feeling as if I am present. It is a form of escapism that I pursue as an act of compulsion.

It is indeed a sickness, and I find it confusing to derive from this yearning that I am indeed an artist, but all facts point to the case that I am. In any case, I am pretty useless at much everything else, so if I must be labelled as such then I am happy to accept that as a descriptor. There was an especially grim episode in my life, soon after one of my particularly bad nervous breakdowns, that I simply disengaged from art altogether. For two years, I refused to even pick up a pencil or paintbrush. Much to the frustration of my family, who could not understand why, as a person who had chosen to attend university purely to study the history of art and had subsequently attended two of the top art schools in the country, I was flat out disassociating myself from all things creative.

The truth was, in that moment, I was absolutely and utterly paralysed with fear. The breakdown from which I was recovering, having left London for a while to recuperate in Dorset at my mother's house, was a particularly brutal one. It happened at my father's house in France, and resulted in me being sectioned in a French psychiatric hospital for around ten days. Time stopped in that place. It just so happens that my French is absolutely second rate, and I was flung into a situation with no means to communicate how I was feeling and absolutely no ability to understand anything about the drugs the staff were administering to me.

Everything was entirely out of my control. I had ended up in those dire straits after having had to be restrained physically by grown men into a gurney, strapped in and shipped off into the rural darkness of vanishing streetlights in the back of an ambulance, in a state of astonishingly high distress. This episode had been building up for weeks, I suppose, but climaxed in me believing I was going to be sent to hell for eternity, where I would be raped forever by the Devil, with razorblades. I was terrified, to such an extent that the adrenaline coursing through my veins gave me superhuman strength, requiring grown men to restrain me.

That place was an eerie and dreadful habitat. Drugged past recognition, I wandered aimlessly about the place, having the same rigmarole of having to swallow hospital food somehow, all the while experiencing a sense of isolation within isolation. This time, not only was I isolated in my illness, but I was also isolated physically, as there was no way I was able to communicate and no way I could understand. Until my father asked my boyfriend at the time to come out to France to visit me, which much to my relief, he did. I do not remember any of his visit. I only remember a glimpse that we were sat down on a bench in the hospital grounds, which looked like a scene from Chernobyl. Other than that, I was far too medicated to be cogent.

So, when I returned to Dorset after this trauma, I was convinced my brain had broken. I was terrified that I had lost the ability to draw, and was far too afraid of making something that would be bad or poorly executed, and therefore proof that I had lost the only thing I was good at and the only reason for me to be alive.

I did not want that to happen.

Sure enough, after two years of holding out, one morning, early, I crept downstairs and into my mother's dining room, where I quietly laid out a sketchpad that had been gathering dust. It was the hardest thing I have ever had to do, to tell myself that I was going to try to make a drawing again. That if I didn't like it, then that was that, and okay, maybe I would have to try again. But in fact, rather marvellously, the image I produced came out to my satisfaction.

I guess it suffices to say that since that drawing, I have not really ever stopped drawing. I went back to art school again, and reconstructed what had at least seemed to be a pretty shattered life up until that point. Those one-year absences of art were very long and very slow, and dragged on as my peers were off living their best lives and I was still trying to recalibrate my brain, rather in havoc after my two psychotic episodes. I had lost my sense of self, my centre axis and my ego in two short but very sharp bursts, and I was forewarned by the psychiatrists that it would take me at least two years to recover. Which was terrible to come to terms with as a 25-or 26-year-old woman. I simply did not have the time or patience to be mentally ill, there was too much to do, a career to be made, love interests to pursue, a shot at the housing market and all the other indicators that you are succeeding as expected in society, according to its set-out milestones.

Of course, to round up this chapter, I must refer to where we began. In escapism. The other pink elephant in the room is the liquid form of escapism that bears the brunt of my own self-loathing, which is of course, alcohol. That is the sure fire, quickest form of escapism from that uncomfortable feeling of a twisted stomach and sense of impending doom that pervades as a result of my condition. This is something I will be approaching in the next chapter, and there are some moments of light relief within the scope of that, such as the fantastic people I have met through fastidiously attending various sobriety groups to curtail or manage my sometimes worrying relationship with booze. I have laughed and cried with these people. I have formed a bond with these other addicts, and people who struggle with various comorbid conditions, that surpasses the usual social decorum and normative sense of friendship. From the aspect of suffering with my condition, where I feel as if I exist on an island far away, and am pretty much destined to be marooned here until the rest of time, at least I have met other damaged people with whom I can exchange a message in a bottle or an SOS call, stuck on their own island in their own environment of isolation. The one redeeming thing I remind myself, is that irrespective of how you feel in that moment of acute loneliness, you are not, in fact, ever alone. And loneliness can be a very unifying and collective sense of togetherness. Perhaps, reader, we can be lonely together?

CHAPTER 4
Supported Accommodation

As I have admitted, I hold a pretty tenuous relation with logical order. My mind ducks and dives between past events, some particularly accented, standing out and taking centre stage, some which fade into the background, and some which seem to resurge more often than others.

A very difficult thing for me to admit, the most troubling time of my life in fact, happened after my relationship with my co-habiting boyfriend broke down irrevocably. I can still feel the twist of his sentence to me, exhaled out in front of my occupational therapist and psychologist, an audience for the most devastating moment of life, as I viewed it at the time. 'I love Lauren but I am not in love with Lauren.' It is utterly besides the point that he had cheated on me twice in the run up to his decapitation of our relationship; I was very much half a person and could not imagine living a life without him. He had picked up the responsibility and load of being almost my carer, as opposed to my lover. The consequence of that sentence, that collection of words set out in that order, meant I had to accept that with the full stop on this relationship, I was now effectively homeless. For the second time in my life.

I have not yet gone back far enough in time relate the first time I became homeless, how I spent around three months in a travellers hostel, sharing a 16-bed dorm each night with strangers and bed bugs. That is to come along in a chapter further into this book. For now, we are going to be looking at what happened next and where I ended up, the people I came across and the various faults with a system of supported accommodation that can be much, much harder to live through, even than a psychiatric unit.

So, we return to the scene in which I heard that explicit sentence, and everything of the past four or so years fell away in an instant. With it, the many good and bad episodes and the prospect of where I believed I was going in my life. Of course, this was all rather delusional. I was in fact still markedly ill, and extremely unhappy in my life and myself, so what that man decided to do on that day was, in retrospect, a favour. But, as it was at the time, within days I suddenly found myself attending an interview along with my reliable occupational therapist, who was attempting to negotiate a space for me in a place for people suffering with acute mental illness. Of course, I was back in a situation I did not want to be in, but a bed was better than no bed. Obviously, as with most things in life, things are never simple. And this place, a house in Whitechapel, did not normally accept bids from 'homeless people', which I had to now accept was my glorified status.

I suppose it worked out; my occupational therapist was a formidable presence in my life and I very much credit her with helping me to recover a semblance of who I am today. I remember that I was there for roughly three weeks, a breathing gap for me in which to regroup somewhat, as a place for me in supported accommodation was arranged. Much of this time passed by in a blur of alcohol. Rather than facing the reality of my predicament, the sedative effect of a can of cider was how I managed what were, at the time, unmanageable emotions. Again, there were people from all walks of life, but for the sake of anonymity I don't think it necessary to go into detail.

41

As it goes, my occupational therapist came up trumps, and wangled me a flat, which I would come to know as my home for the next three years. Three years which have had a seismic impact on me, and for which, had I known how tough they would be, I would never have signed the contract. But how was I to know how it would turn out? This was all new to me, and for that moment I was simply glad to have somewhere to live.

The building was an ugly, redbrick, rectangular building with a baby blue door in the entrance hall. It consisted of two buildings separated by a courtyard garden, shabby at best when I moved in. Years later it would be revamped by a team of strangers volunteering as part of an employees initiative at Barclays bank. That was fairly horrible, as you could feel the stares from these people who held down respectable jobs and gathered a decent income, peering at us all as if we were exhibits in a zoo. Anyway, needs must I suppose. So, with regards to these two buildings, there was an important identifying feature. One of them, the one I was assigned to live in, was for the less ill residents, people with a chance at moving on and out into independent living. The other building, attached to the main building by the entrance hall and communal lounge, was for those residents with a slightly more pessimistic outcome, who would remain there for the foreseeable future.

An important thing to mention before I go on to describe what was a very uncomfortable living experience, is that all of this time, I was enrolled into an art foundation course at an adult education college. Three times a week, I had somewhere to escape to, and I had work to do all the time and briefs to complete and art to be challenged by, which made the reality of my circumstances somewhat bearable. Of course, I still had to attend the weekly residents' meetings every Monday morning.

I actually eased into this social microcosm, some kind of Land of Oz, fairly quickly. As with my account of my time in the psychiatric unit, I will be charting the characters I bumped into here, the various occasions which shaped how I view the way mentally ill people are mistreated by those within the system who are supposed to help aid their recovery, and my formative experience of living with those that society rejects, those that are severely mentally ill, and those who have ventured into criminality as a result of various afflictions of addiction.

I would like to start with Sam. It is a tough pick to begin with, as he was such a troubling character, and there is another man I would like to introduce to you, who along with his friend represent all that is good with mentally ill people. There is also a woman I would like to bring into this story, who I bumped into when I went back to the location years later to check in with people, and found her still there, still not having moved out, still suffering with her illness, which was of course very sad. However, this is the reality for many of these people. Many people do not ever manage to leave supported accommodation, but I digress. So, to return to Sam. Now he was tricky because he was such a damaged soul. Bald and lanky, he approached me straightaway, practically as soon as I had unpacked, and introduced himself to me in a manner in which I assume was meant to impress upon me that *he* was the main guy around the residence.

He appeared to be harmless and charming and unthreatening, so I was all right with being on talking terms with him. I mention Sam as a cautionary tale, as during the course of my three-year stay, he went from someone that may have been troubled but was not enough to break my anxiety threshold, to somebody totally unrecognisable, breaking into the block I lived in throughout the night, banging on doors, begging for money from residents, trying to sell his old and useless electrical equipment for money to fund his ferocious drug habit. It was the drugs that got him in the end. He was eventually kicked out for stealing from another resident, but not before I found out that he had been pimping out another female resident, or the incident where I saw him slap another elderly, vulnerable man across the head. I reported what I had seen straight-away to the staff on duty, but they did not seem bothered by it.

I didn't give up on Sam for a good, long while. Even when he started becoming a rather menacing presence in the residence. At that time in my life I was of the belief that people are all inherently good, though much to the relief of people that care for me I have since reset such a naïve notion and have a healthy amount of protective cynicism. So it came to be that on one occasion, I invited Sam into my flat for him to read his poetry to me. I did not often have visitors to my flat, partly because of the sheer embarrassment of living in such an institution, but also because of the practical constraints on visits, the rules we all had to follow. This meant that any visitor to your flat had to enter through those ugly blue doors, register at reception, and give a 48-hour notice before they arrived. If they were to stay overnight, you were also required to give notice of 48 hours. Simply put, it was all far too much to put upon anyone I knew at the time. The same strict rules applied to me myself in where I was allowed to be. If I was away from my flat for more than 48 hours, the staff would call me and threaten to call the police. So, it was very much an illusion, a false pretence, that you were out of the psychiatric ward and free finally. In the case of this supported accommodation, you were still very much trapped in an oppressive system.

And so Sam was reciting his poetry in my pokey little flat, clutching various notebooks that he must have accumulated over time. He began, voice slightly weak in timbre to begin with, unsure of himself in his expression, tentative with the words he was reading in front of me, sat on my couch as he perched on a chair opposite. The first poem finished. It was fair to middling, above average, there were indeed some tuneful rhymes. It was the content that gave his game away, however. As he shuffled through poem after poem, couplet after couplet, line after line, my understanding of the situation took a turn for the sad. Each poem I had just heard Sam recite was a love song, a sonnet, to heroin. I had just listened through a smorgasbord of incantations to 'Chasing the Dragon', the effects of being high, and the endless beauty of heroin.

I distanced myself from Sam after this recital. I tried to extract myself from being on friendly terms with him and vowed not to invite him into my space henceforth. However, this did not stop him from breaking in on one occasion, when I had a visitor, a handsome man I had met and invited over, much to the consternation of Sam and his burly bully friend Matt, who literally followed this man to my flat, and physically removed him. As far as those two were concerned, as a woman living in the supported accommodation, they laid claim over me as some sort of property of theirs, and therefore had a hand in managing who could come to see me. All rather dramatic really, isn't it?

When your vicinity is based around people who have been forgotten by the world, and you see that abandonment up close, it has a lifelong effect on you. It was all I could do to keep busy during this stage of my life, all I could do to throw myself into various creative projects and work for college. Because if I stopped for a minute to look around me, I may well have fallen to a point from which it would have been inconceivable to get back up again.

As we have learnt so far in my writing style, or lack of anything even approaching a style, I tend to garble my way through paragraphs at great speed without much thought for timelines or you, poor reader. It seems to me that this book is developing into a study of characters I have met since becoming ill. The life I had led up until that point was somewhat more light, and there are parts of my life since which have also been amazing, but the purpose of me sitting with my laptop on my sofa at this moment, approaching one a.m., is to mark out the very serious difficulties I have faced, so that when the time seems right and appropriate, I can pull in some of those positive strands which indicate how far I have come in the journey of my recovery in mental health.

And so, dancing into the frame next, comes our next contender, whom we are going to call Mike. Mike was the very best example of a person tormented by mental illness, yet stoically nice, polite and warm. We all smoked at that residence. Practically everyone there had a daily habit, I had a pretty bad one even at that stage of my life, smoking at least ten Rothmans a day. Now if you know anything about cigarettes, and the hierarchy of brands, you would be aware of the notorious reputation of this particular brand, my brand of choice, within the smoking community and beyond. It is a resolutely disgusting brand. Cheap, nearly as cheap as Mayfair, yet not quite strong enough to feel like you have just inhaled coal dust. In any case, it is a thoroughly unladylike cigarette, and yet I still proudly smoke it as my brand of choice, though hopefully not for too much longer.

I bring up the smoking habit as it was often the time I would interact with Mike and the other residents. The floor of the garden, the concrete and the pebbles, were decorated all the time with discarded cigarette buts, strewn across like confetti from a hard day smoking. Mike was the archetypal mild mannered old man, carrying a hefty pot belly, which almost always seemed to be dressed in the same navy blue jumper. Mike suffered with schizophrenia and would occasionally talk about his life before, enveloped perpetually in the misty blue of cigarette smoke. He was a gentle man, and I suppose I must also state that when I went back to visit that accommodation some years along the line, I saw him still there. I saw him but he did not seem to see me, in all honesty. He did not appear to recognise me, which saddened me somewhat, as I took from that that his condition had markedly deteriorated over the years I had been absent.

So I have catalogued Mike, a benevolent presence for me whilst I stayed there, always happy to hand out a spare cigarette, and an almost permanent feature of the garden. There would be no way to not mention another man, often to be seen in the company of Mike, who I shall refer to as Simon.

The most fascinating thing about Simon was his obsession with numbers. He would recite dates and historical events and show off his prowess with addition and subtraction and all manner of numeracy. It was the thing which would always make him smile, he would often ask you to ask him a number-based question if you saw him, even in passing. Simon was a lovely man. I do not know the extent of his condition, suffice to say it was none of my business. I would also mention that he had a father who would visit him, and so was one of the lucky residents in that respect.

Against this background, I am afraid to say that the culture amongst the support staff was incredibly toxic. There was an overriding power struggle throughout the time that I lived there. I tried to implement constructive change whilst I was there, even something as simple as instating a timetable for the one computer room in the entire building. I had been wrongly informed when I moved for the first year that there was no possibility of having Wi-Fi in my flat, so I would be found in the computer room, on whichever of the two computers was free. That system of organisation did not work, and a total sense of anarchy pervaded the zone.

The difficulty I live with today, the most profound impact of living in such a place, was the total nightmare of staff turnover that was beyond acceptable. Time and time again, I would have to explain my entire life story from scratch, to countless new face after new face. I would attempt in good faith to build up a relationship with the member of staff assigned to me, but this good faith wore off by the tenth time of receiving a full emotional autopsy from yet another stranger. I stopped counting after ten, but I remember the way I was treated by these staff members, which has made it difficult for me to trust mental health professionals. That is obviously a rather long winded way of saying that the standards of care were substandard.

There was one girl I remember in particular. She appears here because she seemed so earnest and steadfast in her dedication to her role, and really even eulogised working for mental health. At the stage she joined the staff, I was totally disillusioned. I just told her straight that she was not going to last in the job, and that I would therefore not be investing so much of myself in her. She was adamant that she was staying; she looked as if she was fresh out of uni and still had that vigorous energy that is mostly only available when you are young, and dissipates with time. Anyway, sure enough, she lasted around six weeks

48

before she quit, and so the endless carousel of new strangers continued on its rotation.

I, too, am guilty of having had an idealised version of how I would be able to change things within that supported accommodation residence. I even told myself, as things progressively disintegrated into yet another manager, that I would return once I had left, or somehow influence how the machine worked. Which is a ridiculous notion, of course - as soon as I did leave, by then utterly worn down, I vowed never ever to return. I consigned it to my past and never talk about it in great depth to anybody. I do remember being furious that when the general election was taking place, there was absolutely no guidance given to the residents. Not one poster reminding them to vote. Not one meeting about how a vote was their right. Not one. It was almost as if the residents were treated as if they did not exist or count, when voting is the one occasion that you have to exist.

Anyhow, the conclusion to this chapter is that I am living independently today, and have been for around five years now. I suppose that even though you move on and life begins to resemble what it looked like before you got ill in the first place, this is in some ways a bit of a chimera, as the time spent in that looming red brick building, has had a transformative impact on my perspective overall. But I try to focus on the fact that I am out of that situation now, and as sad as it is, or rather tragic, that society turns its back on the people who inhabit places like this, they do exist.

CHAPTER 5
Happier Times

And so, dear reader, I thank you for having kept up with me until this point of the story. I imagine we both deserve a break don't you? A vestige of light relief to hiccup along to, after having trawled the bottom of more weighty experiences. For of course, not all life is about pain, especially when you have bipolar disorder. Not all life is pain.

How to box something in? I have been murmuring in my head what to cover in this next chapter, and how to categorise the good times, of which there are indeed so many, so that we feel like we have enjoyed a good meal after this is finished. I was dithering over whether to dedicate a chapter to lovers, or to art school, or to my various dalliances when I first moved to London, or even to go as far back as university days, and the hilarious mish-mash of raves and partying and studying and learning that it was.

Maybe there is a way to glue all of these positive things together as we crash down the slope into my illness, and perhaps that is what we all need right now, an amuse bouche, rather than an aperitif, in order to keep our spirits up?

So, let us start at the top, when I arrived at the sturdy and rather reputable University of Nottingham.

I had been at boarding school for the five years proceeding uni. A very expensive, rather nouveau riche public boarding school in the heart of the Dorset countryside, located near to a quaint, chocolate box town called Wimborne. Wimborne was the kind of place which had its own 'Model Town', the kind of attraction that appeals to a certain demographic, which I hope you can imagine at once. There was a minster, there was even still a Woolworths at that time, I recall. There was a town square that would put up a Christmas tree each year and a lot of those country-style designer clothes shops. There were also a few pubs that would serve underage people, which as you can imagine, made them immensely popular with us, holed away at boarding school much of the time.

I found boarding difficult. I was initially was a day pupil when I started at thirteen, but as my parents moved to Belgium following my dad's posting to the NATO headquarters, I found myself without much choice but to become, all of a sudden, one of the many other girls going through that difficult time of adolescence within the confines of a boarding house.

I digress again. I am sure that period of schooling is a rich theme to return to, but I would rather just lay out the scenario which led to me finally arriving at university, from which I would begin my life of relative freedom.

As is probably very obvious by now, I am terribly disorganised. It is like walking through life with a bit of a wonky limb, you just manage to achieve out of fluke and pure luck. This is what I found out rather quickly within my first term at uni, where I had rather remarkably managed to gain a place to study the history of art. I remember the spectacle of freshers week, I remember the one pound a pint nightclubs, I remember the surprise that, much to my consternation, we humanities students would not be able to just study pure art history, but would have to include modules from other subjects as well, to give us a more rounded education. I always arrived late to the queues for choosing subjects each semester, which is how I ended up studying random modules in courses like philosophy, English lit and French.

During my first year of uni, I caught a case of glandular fever, otherwise known as 'the kissing disease', which I am convinced I caught from an exceptionally handsome hockey player I had a fling with while working as a barmaid at the local hockey club for some extra pocket money. This was much to the consternation of my tutor in art history, who just reckoned that I was falling asleep during lectures out of spite.

And so, uni was a mixture of terrifying and exhilarating. We formed fast friendships in our halls during that first year, and the healthy rivalry of my hall, Cripps, with our neighbouring hall, Hu Stu, was also fun. We all had to pick who we would live with in the second year pretty early on into that first year, which meant that I ended up living my second year of uni (after I had gone back to repeat an exam I had missed so I could actually pass first year, which was a bit silly) with a bunch of girls that I had absolutely nothing in common with, except for one.

It was in second year that I fell in love. Of course, university is a time for sexual liberation. I had enjoyed the company, shall we say, of all kinds of beautiful men during those first twelve months of being eighteen, turning nineteen, and suddenly surrounded by options. But love? No, I had never been in love before, not even with Tom, my best friend from school who spent a lot of his time making me mixtapes of Radiohead and the Postal Service and smoking with me in a romantic haze of teenage love. As it happens, I actually spent more passion on his best friend, Henry, who was notorious as the most intelligent boy at school. He went on to Oxford University, and I actually hung out with him at his freshers week, which was the last time I saw him.

Henry and I would communicate lengthy and meandering love letters to each other over MSN Messenger when I was back home from school in Belgium, and he was wherever he was in the UK. I could never decide who I preferred more, him or Tom? But neither came to anything other than that first stirring of teenage romance.

So, love. I first laid eyes on Adam in his flat in the second year of university. I had met a whole new bunch of friends, who none of my housemates liked or approved of, and one day one of them invited me to Adam's shared flat, which was conveniently just around the corner from my shared house.

It was love at first sight for me. I saw him, this strange looking blonde haired and sculptural impression of a man, laid back in a grotty sofa, in this room full of people who all seemed suddenly very friendly.

One of the people in this room asked me a question, 'So, what school did you go to then?' to which I quipped back, tired after having been asked the exact same question on a fairly boring basis for the entire previous year, 'as if I have not been asked that question a million times before!' To which the room laughed. Of course, as it turned out, this was a room full of very privileged people, all of whom had attended the highest of lofty heights of public boarding schools.

As a line of coke was set up on a mirrored table in the centre of the room, I began to look around me and noticed a fish tank with a strange creature I would later find out was called an axolotl. That was their house guard dog. It was named, 'Vibe Factory'. And so, back to Adam, sat on the sofa, not really saying anything at all whilst other people were munching through conversation, being in the moment. He looked beautiful to me, almost like Adonis, with his shock of wavy blonde hair and contoured face. I pretended not to take much notice of him at all, preferring just to mention him in passing later on to one of the girls who had introduced me to that scene, who politely fed me back that he was indeed single and was indeed very nice.

The chore of being a student at that time was the endless partying at terrible nightclubs. There were three at Nottingham that were notoriously awful. For the purposes of remaining concise, I shall stick to the one where I had my first kiss with said first love, which was called ISIS, and for the duration of the week was a strip club, only to rip off the local student population every Friday by putting on a student night where you could purchase a vodka red bull for a quid.

That is how I fell in love. I kissed Adam on the disgustingly sticky, sweaty dance floor, and from then on we were a thing, much to the consternation of my housemates, who were far too prissy to see what I saw in the man, one of them referring to him as a 'nerd'.

Anyway, I don't really feel like going over too much ground with this, as obviously this first love and I are absolutely no longer in touch. Things ended badly in London when I was working in an art gallery for an absolute dragon. He now has a child and is married, as they all seem to be, with me very much left out of the picture.

So, in order to wrap up this chapter on that first love, I should summarise that it was the beginning of an amazing journey through the rest of university days. Wild parties, put on by this new sparkly set I found myself enjoying being around. All of it was amazing, and it was all such fun.

CHAPTER 6
Getting to Grips with Bipolar Disorder

And so, dear reader, we shall bounce back to the theme of this book, which there is now no getting away from: mental illness. Having felt somewhat like a museum curiosity over the years, asked by myriad people how bipolar disorder affects me, I may as well breathe out a few passages on exactly that. There never really is an appropriate time to ask anybody that kind of question, in all honesty. It is like asking a person with a physical disability, out of the blue, how their disability affects them. However, people seem to want to know the ins and outs, as of course, being mentally ill is not necessarily that common.

I had never known about mental illness growing up. In schooldays we learnt about the dangers of drugs and alcohol in PSHE lessons, and mostly every other variety of dangers to society. I do not recall ever being informed about mental health, however. This is why I felt compelled to go back to my secondary school to give a paper on bipolar disorder and mental illness when I was older.

So it was with pretty much zero knowledge that I absorbed the news of my diagnosis, sat opposite the doctor in the white coat at the first psychiatric unit I had made my temporary home. At that stage in the game, I was still very much manic, I had been making a nuisance of myself for the entire duration of my stay, taking the hideous pictures hung on the corridors off the wall, as they were so truly ugly that they offended me. I was still at this point very much under the belief that I was God, shrugging off the concerned mutterings of staff on the unit who I would overhear saying amongst themselves, 'She is very ill.' I had once pulled off the trick of bartering my way to get a box of matches to light a much needed cigarette, and was rather taken aback when the members of staff told me they thought I was going to attempt to burn down the unit. That thought had never crossed my mind, by the way.

There I am, in a tiny box room, being told this strange new word, to which I responded that if they thought that then okay, but they were agents of the devil, and in actual fact I was Jesus, and there was no way that I had anything wrong with me at all. It was only much later that this diagnosis actually sank in, through repetition over many years, and multiple different psychiatrists. The problem with a label, used to simplify symptoms and people, is that it seems a lazy approach. Taxonomy is useful, as we all like to classify things, especially people, into categories, to make them easier to understand. Things are safe when they are in boxes and groups. Contained. However, where that falls down is in the differences between people who have, like me, received a diagnosis of bipolar disorder.

CHAPTER 7
Depression

What does depression actually feel like? That's the funny thing about depression. It doesn't feel like anything. You don't feel anything. A bee could rock up and sting you and you wouldn't even register it. The funny thing about people, is that they expect you to live a normal life like this. When you cannot face getting out of bed, you're lazy. With their so called helpful advice to go to the gym, when you want to die. I don't say that lightly. I watch my words in a manner that I attribute other people. Depression feels just similar to being on an island.

You are your own hero. You are your own protagonist, You are effectively, your own version, moderated at best, of Robinson Crusoe. And there is nothing you can do about it. You will always have these struggles, and have to laugh along with jokes you don't find funny, as long as they are not at the expense of people you have lived among.

I could write books for days about my experience of mental illness, but dear reader, I wouldn't want to bore you, or grind you down to where I and many others have been. It is a parking lot where nobody can find their car. That is how I would describe it.

CHAPTER 8
Constructing a Reality for the Present Day

So, reader, I hope no offence is taken if I assume we are now close compadres, bearing in mind everything we have covered. I extend a heartfelt mix of gratitude and condolences for having followed me around the storytelling equivalent of the Spaghetti Junction. However, all good things have an ending and each sentence must close in a full stop. More in tune with this trivial little piece of memory-landscaping, I would prefer to end on an ellipsis. So here I am in France, sat down at my father's oversized table, staring into a backdrop of a Sapin Noel I decorated yesterday, trying to tie all of the threads of the previous chapters in a knot, or perhaps more positively a beautiful ribbon bow.

I have not, admittedly, covered so much of the positive happenings, or about how my life happens to be, 'ce moment', as the meaning of this memoir has played out rather more as concise witterings on mental illness, and the beefy, HARDER STUFF, than the light and fluffy cartoon aspects of a life which has surprised myself just as much as anybody else, yourself included, dear reader.

I would not be able to reach a conclusion that I found satisfactory without picking a perfectly timed example of just how far you can get, after losing any recognition of even a semblance of normal life, or of how anybody can recover from trauma. So way back when in this confessional, I included the mortifying case study of being a victim of sexual assault at

Christmas time, a decade ago. It is pure coincidence or, if you are the type to be persuaded by runes and mysticism, serendipity. I remember recounting how I had to collect my belongings like Tom Sawyer, from a gentlemen's club in Mayfair. Specifically, the street just behind the Ritz Hotel, that emblem of luxury and old-world wealth that flies in the face of modern day austerity. There is a scene in the epic Hollywood blockbuster 'Inception' where the streets all fold into themselves and the architecture becomes suffocating and terrifying, and that pretty much sums up the feelings I had at that time, walking away from that stale HQ of aged, most likely impotent and unhappily married men.

To make it make sense, this liaison with meandering yet again, I bring up this street as I was walking along it once again last week. So, in 2022 as opposed to in 2012. I cannot resist adding in the delicious metaphor, that seems so obvious it is probably patronising, though as you know by now, I do display basic bitch tendencies every now and again. That street is not particularly long, but for the purposes of my point, I would say that each 50 metres I walked could be seen as one year in that ten year period since that fall from grace, which I imposed upon myself at the reckoning of somebody else's decision making.

The good thing is that ten years on from that first walk, I was again carrying bags of clothes, but on this occasion, they were the most beautiful, designer clothes. Because I was returning them and other high fashion items to fashion houses or fashion PRs, having assisted an incredibly talented stylist on a fashion shoot for Vogue magazine the previous day. It just so happened that one of the fashion houses on my list of chores for that day had recently moved their headquarters to this street, and so I found myself back in this part of London for the first time in ten years.

Would you like to know what I did when I walked past, on the opposite side of the road, this gentleman's club? I smiled to myself. I broke into a smile and then, quick as anything, I raised my hand and flicked two fingers at this beautiful old building where rancid, old men chose to congregate. I made this gesture with as much gusto as I could, and I loved it, because I was finally getting to reproach the man who raped me. In doing a dream job, in having recovered from what was a pretty dramatic fall, I had and have, bobbed to the surface like a treasure chest sunk at sea.